Public Diplomacy

Edited By
Şeref Ateş and Dr. Melih Barut

Public Diplomacy

Strategic Engagement in Conflicted Communities

PETER LANG

Bibliographic Information published by the Deutsche Nationalbibliothek
The Deutsche Nationalbibliothek lists this publication in the Deutsche
Nationalbibliografie; detailed bibliographic data is available online at
http://dnb.d-nb.de.

Library of Congress Cataloging-in-Publication Data
A CIP catalog record for this book has been applied for at the Library of Congress.

ISBN 978-3-631-76687-3 (Print)
E-ISBN 978-3-631-76688-0 (E-PDF)
E-ISBN 978-3-631-76689-7 (EPUB)
E-ISBN 978-3-631-76690-3 (MOBI)
DOI 10.3726/b14656

© Peter Lang GmbH
Internationaler Verlag der Wissenschaften
Berlin, November 2018
4th edition
All rights reserved.

Peter Lang – Berlin · Bern · Bruxelles · New York · Oxford · Warszawa · Wien

This publication has been peer reviewed.

www.peterlang.com

Table of Contents

Melih Barut

Yunus Emre Institute Cultural Diplomacy Academy

Introduction
Brief Evolutionary History of Diplomacy from Medieval Times to Date and Public Diplomacy Practice for Conflicted Communities

Ever since the ancient ages diplomacy has always been the most important form of communication used by states in the process of shaping their relations with each other for making desired non-conflictual state sustainable while guaranteeing their securities and preserving their national or collective interests without fighting at all levels.

When the historical development and evolution processes of diplomacy is studied, it is observed that the foundations of the classical diplomacy can be traced back to ancient Greece and Rome. In "Iliad" by Homer and "History of the Peloponnesian Wars" by Thucydides, it is possible to come across some certain solid references regarding the early formations of the diplomatic missions, treaties and negotiation culture. Furthermore, in the Roman Empire, which is recognized for their victorious military operations and global conquests throughout the history, it was also observed that they were conducting diplomatic activities for preserving and extending safety as well as security of the Empire.

> *the foundations of the classical diplomacy can be traced back to ancient Greece and Rome. In "Iliad" by Homer and "History of the Peloponnesian Wars" by Thucydides, it is possible to come across some certain solid references regarding the early formations of the diplomatic missions, treaties and negotiation culture.*

The first professional diplomatic organization and foreign affairs department in the modern context has been constituted in the Byzantine Empire in AD 476 in Istanbul right after the collapse of the Roman Empire. Based on this knowledge, it is scientifically possible to correlate the overwhelming success displayed by the Byzantine Empire in their foreign policies in order to extend the life of the Empire under the existing and potential

The first professional diplomatic organization and foreign affairs department in the modern context has been constituted in the Byzantine Empire in AD 476 in Istanbul right after the collapse of the Roman Empire.

threats coming from the East and the West in addition to the internal threats. These amazing efforts exhibited in this particular period by the Byzantine Empire in order to extend the life of the Empire and protect the Empire from the collapse, would later be referred in the history as "the Byzantine Games." So, it can literary be said that the torch of the diplomacy games was lit in the times of the Byzantine Empire.

If we have a look at the evolution of the diplomacy starting from the Byzantine Games to the modern-day diplomacy, in the 15th and 16th Centuries in Europe, we discover that a different version of diplomacy has been rising on unreliable and slippery grounds with intrigue diplomatic operations along with Italian City States. During this period, Niccolò Machiavelli of Florence, who is considered the father of political realism, in his renown work of 1532, "The Prince," he suggests tyrants that killing, encouragement of quarrels among citizens, acquisition of short-term loyalties and betrayal may be permissible when attaining and securing power both in domestic arena as well as in international arena.

As we come closer to the modern diplomatic practices in the evolutionary timeline of diplomacy, politics in the modern terms and traditional understanding of diplomacy in the discipline of international relations are considered officially taken a new form in Europe with the Peace of Westphalia in 1648. It is obvious that with the Peace of Westphalia ending the Thirty Years' wars in Europe, the approach of international system emerged and consequently countries agreed on the following issues leading to the notion of nation states that are in control of their own destiny, sovereign within their borders, independent in their internal affairs, respectful to borders of other states and not interfering their internal affairs, having territorial integrity, abiding to the international conventions they are a part of, and where the relations thereof are managed through mutual diplomatic representations.

The international relations conducted mutually by nation states through bilateral diplomacy after the emergence of international system approach with the Peace of Westphalia of 1648 reached a new dimension with the Treaty of Vienna (Congress of Vienna) of 1815. The Congress of Vienna convened in order to establish the balance of powers which was turned upside down in Europe as a result of the 1789 French Revolution and the Napoleonic Wars. In addition to that, the Congress of Vienna was also summoned to embrace an awareness for empowering international relations of nation states by means of multilateral diplomatic relations to be conducted simultaneously with bilateral ones. In this context, it is also noted in the Congress of Vienna, where for the first time a multi-will was voiced for establishment of a collective security system in European continent, that significant structural arrangements were made and inured in the approach of international diplomatic representation the foundations of which had been laid in with the Peace of Westphalia. In this regard, the foundations of the principles pertaining to the extents and formations of traditional diplomatic missions generally in the sense presently used have been laid in the Treaty of Vienna of 1815.

The foundations of the traditional diplomacy in the sense we utilize today were laid as per the Act on the Priorities of Diplomatic Constituents (64 CTS 453) agreed upon during the Congress of Vienna on 9th June 1815 abiding by the spirit of the Peace of Westphalia of 1648. Over the period of past 200 years, although applicable details of the traditional diplomacy approach were tried to be reformed through the arrangements reforming the diplomatic relations, such as primarily the Treaty of Vienna of 18 April 1961, the fundamentals determined in the Congress of Vienna of 1815 have been considered as the basic guiding principles.

Although it is found out that there was not much change or transformation involved in the primary reasons requiring the use of diplomacy, it is also discovered that alternative new diplomacy methods were developed and used by state actors for paving the way for traditional diplomacy in so many arenas in order to secure their own national or collective interests. When the reason behind the need for alternative diplomacy in addition to the traditional diplomacy is analyzed, it is discovered that alternative diplomacy is required as an emergency exit, when traditional diplomacy reached to a dead end. There are many forms of alternative diplomacy which are designed for reengaging the state actors in the times of diplomatic crises. In this context, public diplomacy can be regarded as the most crucial way of reconnecting state actors and can be defined as the diplomatic efforts conducted form governments to the foreign public audiences with the objective of bringing the multidimensional

alternative diplomacy is required as an emergency exit, when traditional diplomacy reached to a dead end.

> *public diplomacy can be regarded as the most crucial way of reconnecting state actors and can be defined as the diplomatic efforts conducted form governments to the foreign public audiences with the objective of bringing the multidimensional differences together on a common ground and opening space for the progress of traditional diplomacy through common social, cultural and humanitarian values.*

differences together on a common ground and opening space for the progress of traditional diplomacy through common social, cultural and humanitarian values. It is also believed that the comprehensive public diplomacy efforts exhibited in potentially conflicted regions would help the prevention of the minor crisis before they transform into bigger crisis by bringing the people of conflicts closer to each other. In this way, continuity in preemptive engagement will be sustained through public diplomacy efforts, which places culture, education, science, sport, history, music, language and fine arts into the heart of the engagement strategy.

This book compiles contributions presented at the conference on **"The Role of Public Diplomacy in Bringing the Conflicted Communities Together,"** which was organized by Yunus Emre Institute Cultural Diplomacy Academy and Global Public Diplomacy Network and through the valuable contributions of globally recognized academics, diplomats and practitioners from around the world. Yunus Emre Institute Cultural Diplomacy Academy as for the primary organizer of this international conference took the initiative of turning the presentations and panel discussions into a book with the objective of spreading the valuable contributions provided by the distinguished participants to the wider global audience.

The contributions to the conference are covered in the book in two parts. While the first part of the book contains the speeches delivered by the contributors, the second part includes the panel discussion. The first part of the book starts with the opening speech delivered by President of Yunus Emre Institute, Professor Şeref Ateş. In his speech, Professor Ateş explores **"The Role of Yunus Emre Institute and Global Public Diplomacy Network in Promoting Global Peace, Harmony and Social Cohesion."**

Professor Brigitte Nacos from Columbia University gives some insights about **"A New Public Diplomacy for the 21st Century."** In her keynote speech, she provides some solid hands-on guidance to public and cultural diplomats that would bring conflicted communities together.

Professor Bekir Karlığa from the United Nations Alliance of Civilizations National Coordination Committee discusses the necessity of the **"The New Understanding of Civilization for Global Peace, Security and Prosperity."** In his talk, Professor Karlığa provides various alternative solutions to the problems tearing the East and the West apart from each other by elaborating conflictual background in historical context.

Ambassador Luan Starova from Macedonia takes culture as the common ground where humanitarian values would rise together. Ambassador Starova declares in his talk entitled **"Cultural Diplomacy for Humanity's Common Benefit"** that the role of cultural diplomacy is to establish a harmony between differences by emphasizing cultural and humanitarian values that feed on the same or similar roots in this global mentality.

Ambassador Luis Palma Castillo from the Ministry of National Defense of Chile in his talk entitled **"Social Media in Public Diplomacy as a Leverage to Traditional Diplomacy"** explores the role of social media in public diplomacy as a support element to traditional diplomatic efforts.

The second part of the book covers the panel discussion on **"The Future and the Role of Public Diplomacy in Conflict Prevention."** The panel explores the basic conflictual issues among Eastern and Western societies with a special focus on the current and future role of public diplomacy in the prevention of the existing as well as potential conflicts. The panel is moderated by Coordinator of Yunus Emre Institute Cultural Diplomacy Academy Dr. Melih Barut and it is successfully executed with the valuable contributions of Professor Brigitte Nacos, Professor Bekir Kalığa and Ambassador Luis Palma Castillo.

This book highlights the Eastern and the Western perspectives on diplomacy in general and public diplomacy as well as the use of public diplomacy in conflict prevention processes in particular. Furthermore, it mainly focuses on the practical hands-on applications of the public diplomacy in the field rather than generating a new academic discourse in the field of public diplomacy. In that sense, we believe that this book can provide guidance to the diplomats, public diplomacy experts, cultural diplomats and to strategic communicators in their quest for hands-on solutions in the field.

Notes on Contributors

Şeref Ateş

Şeref Ateş received his first Ph.D. from the Department of Western Languages and Literature: German Language and Literature, at Ankara University and his second Ph.D. from the Department of Political Science at University of Marburg, Germany. With the foundation of Yunus Emre Institute in 2009, Ateş was appointed General Manager of the Centre for Learning Turkish and Coordinator of Yunus Emre Institutes in Europe. In 2013, Ateş was appointed Vice Chairman of the Yunus Emre Institute and served in this role for three years. Dr. Şeref Ateş's areas of expertise and research include international relations, cultural diplomacy, media and communications, translation science, multiculturalism, the relationship between culture and politics, teaching Turkish as a second language and non-governmental organizations. Published nationally and internationally, Ateş currently serves as the president of Yunus Emre Institute and Chairman of the Global Public Diplomacy Network. He is also the founder and global advocate of Academic and Scientific Cooperation Project of Turkey (TABIP)

Brigitte L. Nacos

Brigitte L. Nacos is a journalist and political scientist. She received her Ph.D. from Columbia University, where she teaches in the Department of Political Science on mass media, public opinion, decision-making and social movements. Based on her major research interest, she also holds courses on terrorism, counterterrorism, and the centrality of communication and publicity in the terrorist calculus. Her most recent books are "Terrorism and Counterterrorism," Fifth Edition (2016) and "Mass-Mediated Terrorism: Mainstream and Digital Media in Terrorism and Counterterrorism," Third Edition (2016).

Bekir Karlığa

Head of the United Nations Alliance of Civilizations National Coordination Committee and former senior advisor to the prime minister of Turkey, Bekir Karlığa received his Ph.D. from Istanbul University with the dissertation entitled "Pythagoras and Pre-Socratic Philosophers in the light of Islamic Resources and Philosophers." Lecturing for multiple years on Islamic philosophy, comparative East-West philosophy and history of civilizations,

Dr. Bekir Karlığa has published more than 50 books. Lately, he has intensified all his efforts on a documentary project known as "The River Flowing Westward - Batıya Akan Nehir." The award-winning documentary shot in 16 different countries with the direct contributions of more than 200 experts from different nationalities and various academic fields rejects the "clash of civilizations thesis," aims to inform audience about the rich science, thought, art and civilizational heritage which the East and the Islamic world transferred to the West.

Luan Starova

Luan Starova is a writer and diplomat. He received his Ph.D. in French and Comparative Literature. He subsequently worked as a professor of French Literature at the University of Skopje. In the 1990s, he served as the first ambassador of the Republic of Macedonia in Paris. He is the author of novels, poetry and essays, as well as of translations of French writers into Macedonian. Starova, who is a member of the Macedonian Academy of Arts and Sciences, writes and publishes both in his native Albanian and in Macedonian. Among Luan Starova's major novels are "Tatkovite knigi" ("My Father's Books"), Skopje 1992, published in Albanian as "Librat e babait," Skopje 1995; "Koha e dhive" ("The Age of the Goat"), 1993, published in Macedonian as "Vremeto na kozite," Skopje 1993; and "Ateisticki muzej" ("The Museum of Atheism"), Skopje 1997. His works have also become widely available in French, German, Italian, Turkish, Romanian, Croatian, Bulgarian and Greek.

Luis Palma Castillo

Luis Palma Castillo was thirty-six years in the Chilean foreign service. He was posted in South Africa, Israel, twice in the United Kingdom, Canada and Ecuador. He was appointed ambassador to the Hashemite Kingdom of Jordan, accredited in the Kingdom of Saudi Arabia, and later, he served as ambassador to Turkey, accredited to the Islamic Republic of Pakistan. By profession, he is a teacher of history and geography and holds a Master's degree in Political Science from the Catholic University of Santiago, Chile. He also received a Master of Arts in International Affairs from Carleton University, Ottawa, Canada. He has taught world politics at many universities and academic institutions in Chile. Ambassador Palma has written many papers regarding historic events in the Middle East, such as; "Gallipoli 1915, 100 years"; he also wrote the book; "The Ideological Confrontation between the USA and the Soviet Union", co-authored with

Dr. Gilberto Aranda "The Middle East an Eternal Crossroad" and "The Crepuscular Aurora of the Middle East." Currently, he is an international affairs advisor at the Ministry of National Defense.

Melih Barut

Melih Barut is the founding coordinator of Yunus Emre Institute Cultural Diplomacy Academy and the Secretary-General of Global Public Diplomacy Network under Yunus Emre Institute presidency. His professional, academic and active research expertise includes: strategic communication, terrorism and counterterrorism, political digital media analysis, social movements, contentious politics, integrity building, civilian and military relations, military diplomacy, public diplomacy and cultural diplomacy. Dr. Melih Barut has lectured at many leading international military and civic institutions around the world. He regularly lectures at the NATO Center of Excellence Defense Against Terrorism and Turkish General Staff Partnership for Peace Training Center. Barut was also as a research scholar at Columbia University's Department of Political Science, where he explored the impact of digital media on contentious politics to support his doctoral dissertation.

Part One

Şeref Ateş, Yunus Emre Institute

Şeref Ateş

Yunus Emre Institute

Chapter 1
The Role of Yunus Emre Institute and Global Public Diplomacy Network (Gpdnet) in Promoting Global Peace, Harmony and Social Cohesion

Abstract: Public Diplomacy has emerged as a popular discipline over the last few years supporting the traditional diplomacy which is run by the governments in many aspects. The latest advances in Internet & Information and Communication Technologies (ICTs) domains are directly or indirectly affecting the social structure of the global society and the rules of digital social engagement with the foreign public through Public Diplomacy, Cultural Diplomacy and Strategic Communication. The chapter explores the role of Yunus Emre Institute and Global Public Diplomacy Network in minimizing the potential of cross-cultural conflicts.

Keywords: Public Diplomacy, Cultural Diplomacy, Social Engagement, Yunus Emre Institute, Global Public Diplomacy Network, Conflict

The old planet that we all live on has been transformed with an incredible speed over the last two decades and this transformation process has been accelerating in an amazing rate for a long time. The reason behind this rapid transformation which is observed in almost every field can be partially explained by the groundbreaking advances that the global society is witnessing in the domains of the Internet as well as Information and Communication Technologies (ICTs). It is also observed that the advances in the Internet & ICTs domains directly and indirectly affected the social structure of the global society. Currently, we are living in a Network Society where global interaction between the citizens of the world is at its peak point. As communication science scholar Manuel Castells puts it in his book entitled *Network Society*, this new type of society, which he names it "Network Society", is "a society whose social structure is made up of networks powered by micro-electronics-based information and communications technologies" (2004 p. 3). As Castells highlights in his book, throughout the history there have always been social networks, however the critical factor that distinguishes the network society from the previous ones is that the impact of ICTs on the creation and sustainment of remote networks in which new types of interactive social relationships are created.

This simply means that fates of the societies and countries are more bound together than ever before. It is believed that this situation would bring the potential of struggle among the state and non-state actors over the conflicting interests. In addition to that, it is also believed that Post-Westphalian conventional diplomacy tools, dealing with the sophisticated and interrelated sets of global issues, ranging from stability and migration, global security and climate change, sectarian violence and international terrorism, and the list goes on and on, would not be capable enough to develop multiple alternate solutions to the prevention of the existing and potential conflicts in the world.

> *international affairs scholars are strictly criticizing the Post-Westphalian diplomacy understanding. And they are simultaneously trying to expand the area of influence of conventional diplomacy in order to transform and empower it, so as to be more proactive in the process of the prevention of potential global, regional and local crisis.*

Today, we are witnessing that some international affairs scholars are strictly criticizing the Post-Westphalian diplomacy understanding. And they are simultaneously trying to expand the area of influence of conventional diplomacy in order to transform and empower it, so as to be more proactive in the process of the prevention of potential global, regional and local crisis. Now, in the world of academia there is an ongoing debate over the different forms of diplomacy and their potential implications, which is basically seeking the best possible form of diplomacy which fulfills the requirements of network society of the 21st Century. It seems that the majority of the scholars have reached some kind of agreement on the comprehensive diplomacy or integrative diplomacy, which locates the strategic communication efforts in the core and simply

> *Now, in the world of academia there is an ongoing debate over the different forms of diplomacy and their potential implications, which is basically seeking the best possible form of diplomacy which fulfills the requirements of network society of the 21st Century.*

It seems that the majority of the scholars have reached some kind of agreement on the comprehensive diplomacy or integrative diplomacy, which locates the strategic communication efforts in the core and simply benefits from the synchronized use of all forms of diplomacy including public and cultural diplomacy.

benefits from the synchronized use of all forms of diplomacy including public and cultural diplomacy.

In line with the transforming nature of the conventional diplomacy, Yunus Emre Institute--Cultural Diplomacy Agency of Turkey, promotes wider knowledge of Turkey, Turkish language, Turkish culture, Turkish history, Turkish music, fine arts and science in the country and around the world. Shortly, the Institute promotes all belonging to the culture of these ancient lands which are also referred to as the cradle of the civilizations. Yunus Emre Institute, all around the world is intensifying its efforts to the solutions of the problems fostering potential local, regional and global conflicts. While doing that Yunus Emre Institute embraces the teachings of the 13th-Century Anatolian Phi-

Yunus Emre Institute--Cultural Diplomacy Agency of Turkey, promotes wider knowledge of Turkey, Turkish language, Turkish culture, Turkish history, Turkish music, fine arts and science in the country and around the world. Shortly, the Institute promotes all belonging to the culture of these ancient lands which are also referred to as the cradle of the civilizations.

losopher Yunus Emre and his wisdom as a guidance.

It is believed that the following verse of Yunus Emre explains the philosophy and philanthropy of Yunus Emre Institute, its global expansion policy as well as Institutes' attitude in bringing the conflicted communities together.

> Come, let us all be friends for once,
> Let us make life easy on us,
> Let us be lovers and loved ones,
> The earth shall be left to no one.[1]

It should also be noted that Yunus Emre's teachings are not the only guidance that the Institute embraced in quest of local, regional and global peace and harmony. In that sense the teachings of Grand Anatolian Culture

---

1   Halman, T., & Findikoğlu, Z. (2009). *Popular Turkish Love Lyrics and Folk Legends* (Warner J., Ed.). Syracuse, NY: Syracuse University Press.

should be recognized in this particular point. Anatolia, or as the western scholars call it Asia Minor, has always been regarded as the crossroads of the civilizations. Anatolia is one of the oldest continuously inhabited regions in the world and the history of Anatolia stretches far back to the Neolithic period. In that context, archeological researches tell us that Çatalhöyük region is one of the earliest human settlements in Anatolia and archaeologists claim that the settlement lasted from 7500 BC to 5700 BC. When the time span from 7500 BC to the day taken into account together with the ancient civilizations settled on these lands, it could be easily understood where the rich Anatolian unity of the diversities culture comes from and how the mutual respect oriented Anatolian coexistence practice was formed.

Yunus Emre Institute, backed both by the philanthropy of Yunus Emre in his teachings and the wisdom of Anatolian cultural heritage inherited from the Anatolian civilizations, today displaying continuous efforts in order to spread peace, harmony and social prosperity to the whole world in the form of cultural diplomacy. Up until now as an institute we are conducting our cultural diplomacy activities with our Cultural Diplomats in 40 countries with more than 50 centers, universities and branch offices. Inspired from following verse of Yunus Emre, the Institute is expanding in each year.

I didn't come to create any problems,
I'm only here to love.
A Heart makes a good home for the Friend.
I've come to build some hearts.[2]

Based on the mutual belief that public and cultural diplomacy contributes to the creation of innovative policy-oriented solutions to the issues affecting many countries, the Global Public Diplomacy Network (GPDNet) is founded as a multilateral platform. GPDNet contributes to international community through cultural and civil society initiatives by sharing knowledge and encouraging cooperation.

In addition to the individual efforts, Yunus Emre Institute is also taking active roles in global alliances as in the case of Global Public Diplomacy Network. Based on the mutual belief that public and cultural diplomacy contributes to the creation of innovative policy-oriented solutions to the issues affecting many

2   Halman, T., & Başgöz, İ. (1981). *Yunus Emre and His Mystical Poetry*. Indiana: Indiana University Press.

countries, the Global Public Diplomacy Network (GPDNet) is founded as a multilateral platform. GPDNet contributes to international community through cultural and civil society initiatives by sharing knowledge and encouraging cooperation.

The GPDNet is comprised of non-profit national level institutions promoting cultural and public diplomacy. Yunus Emre Institute is the founding member of GPDNet and holding the term presidency since 1ˢᵗ July, 2016 for three years.

In line with the vision of GPDNet, members strive to promote (but not limited to) the following collaborative activities:

- Organize conferences, seminars, workshops and other educational events related to the exchange of knowledge and experience in the field of public diplomacy
- Encourage collaboration in the visual arts, exhibitions, performances and publication sector to expand public awareness of culture
- Promote people-to-people exchanges to enhance mutual understanding and trust; and
- Organize joint training programs and personnel exchange to strengthen ties between Members.

Upon the handover of the term presidency to Yunus Emre Institute, the following major projects are executed in cooperation with other GPDNet members with the objective of promoting cross-cultural communication, global peace and harmony among the peoples of the member countries.

First International conference of GPDNet is performed with the support of Yunus Emre Institute Cultural Diplomacy Academy which was activated in 2017 with the objective of training and educating the cultural diplomats who will be assigned to various locations in the world. The GPDNet International conference is basically concentrated on the "The Role of Public Diplomacy in Bringing Conflicted Communities Together". The conference is followed by a panel discussion where the "The Future of the Public Diplomacy and the Role of Public Diplomacy in Conflict Prevention" is discussed.

As it has been put forward, Yunus Emre Institute, empowered by the teachings of Anatolian philosophers and by the wisdom of Anatolian cultural heritage, is making use of every possible opportunity for promoting and spreading peace, harmony and social prosperity all around the world in order to minimize the potential of cross cultural conflicts while maximizing the mutual understanding.

Brigitte L. Nacos, Columbia University

Brigitte L. Nacos

Columbia University

Chapter 2
A New Public Diplomacy for the 21ˢᵗ Century

Abstract: The post-Cold War prospect of a "New World Order" raised the expectations of a global community of nations living together without any major conflicts and great wars. However, while the Internet and digital social networks created social platforms for the engagement of people coming from different political social, cultural, religious and ethnic background, the messages shared both through the conventional media and through social media platforms are perceived and interpreted very differently by different people in different political, cultural, and religious settings in different parts of the world. This chapter explores how divisive communication processes can be improved through public diplomacy by minimizing the potential conflicts with the objective of bringing conflicted communities together both in virtual and actual environments.

Keywords: New World Order, Public Diplomacy, Stereotypes, Terrorism, Mass Media, Social Media, Conflicts

Half a century ago, the advances in communication technology led the Canadian philosopher Marshall McLuhan to imagine the future as a "global village" where information would move instantaneously from one place in the world to any other location. While McLuhan himself did not predict a unified, tranquil, conflict-free global village, other futurists assumed that more information about the world and each other would bring people of different geographic locations, cultures, races, religions, socio-economic status, etc., to understand each other better.

The revolution in information and communication technology and the rise of digital communication came more speedily than even McLuhan could have imagined. Similarly dramatic were the changes in the geopolitical landscape in the aftermath of the Cold War.

The notion of a "New World Order" fueled expectations of a global community of nations living without the major conflicts and without great wars. Francis Fukuyama told us in the early 1990s that the world reached "The End of History" since capitalism and democracy had triumphed and became the models for modernizing countries "linked with one another through global markets and the spread of a universal consumer culture."

What a thought: The world would be a more or less harmonious place because we all would be content to share food, blue jeans, sit-coms, and Hollywood blockbusters. It did not turn out that way.

The scholar Benjamin Barber got it right. He recognized quite early that the global reach of entertainment and news media along with widely promoted and distributed consumer goods dominated by the West and especially the United States—did not result in a new kind of world citizen, but rather fueled alienation and resentment amongst people and communities in the advanced and developing world who see their cultures, values, traditions and religions threatened and crowded out by alien intruders.

Never before in history has information been available to more people more speedily and more affordable than today.

Never before in history has information been available to more people more speedily and more affordable than to-day. It is difficult to imagine our professional lives without the computer and the wealth of information available on the World Wide Web. Taken together, I have spent many months, years in libraries to research material that I now can easily access from my computer at home or in the office. In our private lives, we can at all times keep in touch with family and friends regardless of the distances between us. That's the up-side.

At first sight, the up-side is, too, that news and entertainment are "broadcast" by global TV-networks, Internet sites, and social media platforms in the sense of being available to people all around the globe. But the same news message, the same television image, the same film narrative can be and is perceived very differently by different people in different political, cultural and religious settings.

the same news message, the same television image, the same film narrative can be and is perceived very differently by different people in different political, cultural and religious settings.

When Western leaders speak of the "war on terrorism," many Westerners are likely to think of terrorists of the Al Qaeda or ISIS variety. Many Muslims, among them many in the Western diaspora, are likely to think that the "war on terrorism" is a code word for "war against Islam." The same words, the same terms—very different perceptions!

Instead of the imagined electronic global meeting halls, where we learn about and respect each other's cultures, traditions and values, we have something like an electronic Tower of Babel with different tribes thinking and speaking and acting differently—unable to engage in meaningful people-to-people exchanges. This state of affairs makes for conflicts—often deadly conflicts.

Think of the Danish cartoons and similar images in the French satirical magazine *Charlie Hebdo*. Publishing those demeaning depictions of the Prophet Muhammad caused severe crises and deaths. Not for all, but for many Westerners those images were offensive, in bad taste, and shouldn't have been published. But there was also an understanding that freedom of expression and freedom of the press should not be interfered with. For many Muslims in those two countries and even more so in Muslim majority countries the publication of those cartoons came down to blasphemy, was an insult of and an attack on their deep seated religious convictions. Why, they asked, didn't the Danish and French authorities punish those responsible? Why didn't the authorities apply their laws against hate speech?

Attempts to open meaningful dialogues could have resulted in a better understanding between political leaders on the one hand and Muslim leaders on the other hand for the benefit of all the people. For that to happen, both sides needed to know each other's different cultural, religious, and political traditions, their values and sensitivities. There was a lack of knowledge based on shared experiences, conversations, explanations. There was even less relevant knowledge among the broad publics on either side. The divide eventually led to violence and deaths that I think could have been prevented—by both traditional diplomacy and public diplomacy.

> *Knowledge of and respect for different cultures and polities and religions must be the foremost goal in efforts to bring conflictual communities together.*

Knowledge of and respect for different cultures and polities and religions must be the foremost goal in efforts to bring conflictual communities together. Thus, the question: What kind of Public Diplomacy (PD) is most promising in the second decade of the 21st century and beyond?

The traditional PD model for governments and NGOs to engage with foreign publics was based on three major pillars:

- Government directed information that promotes the nation's values and policies has always been number one effort—followed by
- Cultural exchange programs promoting language, culture, science, arts, sports

- Educational People-to-People Contacts—especially among students, scholars, business people.

Through most of the 20th century it made sense for the first pillar—information—to be the most important of the three approaches. In the past, there were still mostly national spheres of communication—print and broadcast. To be sure, there were wire services, foreign correspondents, there were telephone connections, radio and TV networks that reached beyond national borders, especially when satellite transmissions came around. But there was no instant transmission of information on a global scale. There was mass communication, but not yet today's truly global information and communication systems of mass communication plus what Manuel Castells calls mass self-communication[3].

While some perceptive diplomats and academics recognized after the end of the Cold War and even more so in the early 21st century that there was the need for a new public diplomacy model, most politicians and career bureaucrats remained stuck in the past. After the Cold War was over and the advent of the so-called "New World Order" was celebrated, public diplomacy was no longer seen as an important part of government-to-foreign-publics diplomacy.

Indeed, in the late 1990s, during the Bill Clinton presidency, the United States Information Agency (USIA) was dismantled and its underfunded skeleton folded into the US Department of State with the broadcasting components becoming a freestanding agency. That was a bitter end for an agency whose "soft power" approach contributed to the de-escalation of many Cold-War crises, most of all the Cuban Missile Crisis.

After the attacks of 9/11, public diplomacy became part of Washington's "war on terrorism" strategy. Those in charge put their chips on traditional Madison Avenue marketing and branding approaches. Then U.S. Secretary of State Colin Powell hired a Madison Avenue executive as Undersecretary for Public Diplomacy. He chose the branding specialist as Powell explained to brand the United States as successfully as this branding expert had branded and sold Uncle Ben's Rice, Head and Shoulders Shampoo and other consumer goods.

---

3 CASTELLS, Manuel. Communication, Power and Counter-power in the Network Society. International Journal of Communication, [S.l.], v. 1, p. 29, Feb. 2007. ISSN 1932–8036.

It was a time when traumatized Americans asked in the wake of the most horrific terrorist attack, "Why do they hate us?" The glitzy PD campaign a la Madison Avenue designed to win over Arabs and Muslims in the Middle East flopped. Ads and commercials depicting Muslim Americans appreciative of and happy with their lives in America became a laughing stock in targeted populations. People knew about the difficult predicaments of Muslims in post-9/11 America. Perhaps this sort of marketing could have succeeded in the past; it was not credible in the age of global information and communication.

One of the most esteemed American newsman, Edward R. Murrow, who at the end of his career headed up the United States Information Agency, said of what was then still called "propaganda"—not public diplomacy or soft power:

- To be persuasive we must be believable;
- To be believable, we must be credible;
- To be credible, we must be truthful;
- It is a simple as that.

It may be as simple as that--but this is not how public diplomacy is always practiced. It was not practiced in Murrow's sense in Washington's post-9/11 public diplomacy—or better—marketing campaigns.

I believe that a foremost goal of public diplomacy must be an offensive against stereotypes. If the first pillar of public diplomacy, the dissemination of advocacy information cannot do the job, one wonders about the roles and effects of the traditional mass media and the new social media. Unfortunately, the latter are unlikely vehicles to weaken or eradicate stereotypes that vilify people of different nationalities, religions, and races.

> *foremost goal of public diplomacy must be an offensive against stereotypes.*

We know from the researches that news and entertainment media reinforce deep-seated cultural stereotypes that divide, not unite people. Take Western stereotypes about Muslims and Arabs. Following the Iran hostage crisis, Columbia University professor Edward Said, a leading scholar on the Middle East, made a great point in his book "Covering Islam: How the Media and the Experts Determine How We See the Rest of the World":

> *news and entertainment media reinforce deep-seated cultural stereotypes that divide, not unite people.*

"Muslim and Arabs are essentially covered [in the news], discussed, appre-
hended either as oil suppliers or as potential terrorists. Very little of the detail,
the human density, the passion of Arab-Muslim life has entered the awareness
of even those people whose profession it is to report the Islamic world."[4]

*Bad news dominates in the news
media—the good and positive is not or
rarely reported. And social media, too,
magnifies the bad, not the good.*

Bad news dominates in the
news media—the good and
positive is not or rarely reported. And social media,
too, magnifies the bad, not
the good. This distorts real-
ity and affirms what Walter Lippmann told us nearly 100 years ago: News
is not truth. As I like to explain it to my students, news is merely a small
slice from the whole pie of reality and truth.

Jack Shaheen, the author of "Arab and Muslim Stereotypes in American Popular Culture"[5] and "Reel Bad Arabs: How Hollywood Vilifies a
People"[6] analyzed all Hollywood films throughout the history that featured
Arabs and/or Muslims. His conclusion was that in motion pictures Arabs
and Muslims were and still are predominantly fanatics, violent, lazy, non-
cultured—and in more recent times terrorists.

Reeva Simon in "The Middle East in Crime Fiction" recognized links between bad news and fiction. She wrote, before 9/11—it is not better today.

"Middle Easterners will continue to populate the casts of villains and conspirators in popular fiction because authors know that today, after watching
the evening news and reports of bombed American embassies, kidnapped or
killed diplomats, and the latest exploits of religious fanatics, the public will
readily read about Middle Eastern conspirators and that books about the
area will sell."[7]

Nobody has described the origin and power of stereotypes more compel-
lingly than Lippmann.

---

4   Said, E. W. (1997). Covering Islam: How the media and the experts determine
    how we see the rest of the world. New York: Vintage Books.
5   Shaheen, J. G. (2004). Arab and Muslim stereotyping in American popular
    culture. Washington: Walsh school of foreign services.
6   Shaheen, J. G. (2015). Reel bad Arabs: How Hollywood vilifies a people. North-
    ampton, Massachusetts: Olive Branch Press.
7   Simon, R. S. (1989). The Middle East in Crime Fiction: Mysteries, Spy Novels
    and Thrillers from 1916 to the 1980s. New York: Lilian Barber Pr.

West-Eastern Divan Orchestra www.west-eastern-divan.org

"In the great blooming, buzzing confusion of the outer world we pick out what our culture has already defined for us and we tend to perceive that which we have picked out in the form stereotypes for us by our culture," he wrote. "The subtlest and most pervasive of all influences are those which create and maintain the repertoire of stereotypes."[8]

Lippmann recognized that only education and knowledge could overcome stereotypical thinking and acting.

The most important point here is that in all societies, among all ethnic, racial, religious groupings stereotypes about "the other" are part of cultural perceptions and tend to be reinforced by both news and entertainment media. Some are positive — most are negative, and they are not weakened by the content of news media, entertainment media, social media or government info campaigns.

Therefore, public diplomacy must move the second and third pillars of its triad mentioned above to the front burner and focus most of all on cultural learning and exchanges and collaborative projects. Most of what we know about the world, most of what we know about people abroad is second-hand knowledge. Needed is first-hand knowledge–about other

---

8   Lippmann, W. (1997). Public Opinion. New York: Routledge.

peoples, other cultures, other religions, other values. Tourism is a good thing but not enough to fill the cultural knowledge gap.

We need more people-to-people gatherings like we experience at this conference, exchanging and sharing ideas, research, expertise, working together towards goals we can agree on—and yes, breaking bread together as well. Collaborative projects result in more and shared knowledge and understanding.

We need more people-to-people gatherings like we experience at this conference, exchanging and sharing ideas, research, expertise, working together towards goals we can agree on—and yes, breaking bread together as well. Collaborative projects result in more and shared knowledge and understanding. One of the most unlikely and most successful examples here is the "West-Eastern Divan Orchestra" for young people founded 18 years ago by Palestinian-American Edward Said and Jewish conductor Daniel Barenboim with the goal to bring young musicians from Palestine and Israel together on neutral ground to make music together, to get to know each other, to think about peace. The first workshop in Weimar, Germany, was perceived as a one-time collaborative project. The collaboration never ended. It is blossoming. Every summer a new workshop brings together young Arab, Muslim, Jewish musicians in Spain for rehearsals, for discussions, for mutual learning. The orchestra gives concerts around the world. In October 2017, there were much celebrated performances in London, Paris, and Berlin. Referring to a colleague in the orchestra an Egyptian Violinist Mini Zikri said:

> "Images can be very misleading. The suicide bomber brings to mind a certain image, so does the military operation. But these must not be fixed in one's brain. Now when I see her again I think, 'Here is my friend,' not 'Here is the Israeli person.'"[9]

---

9   Cowan G and Arsenault A (2008) Moving from monologue to dialogue to collaboration: The three layers of public diplomacy. The Annals of the American Academy of Political and Social Science, 616(1), pp. 10–30 Academic papers

We need more such collaborative projects. We need more cultural people-to-people exchanges and initiatives. That must be the core of the 21st century PD: Cultural Public Diplomacy. Knowing more about different cultures and histories and peoples and races and religions based on personal experiences, meetings, and collaborations will not prevent disagreements, but can help to understand others and temper our actions and reactions.

> *Knowing more about different cultures and histories and peoples and races and religions based on personal experiences, meetings, and collaborations will not prevent disagreements, but can help to understand others and temper our actions and reactions.*

Bekir Karlığa, United Nations Alliance of Civilizations, National Coordination Committee

Bekir Karlığa

United Nations Alliance of Civilizations
National Coordination Committee

Chapter 3
The New Understanding of Civilization for Global Peace, Security and Prosperity

Abstract: Conflicts, disagreements, fights and wars lie in the deep roots of the history. When the conflicts and kinetic and non-kinetic wars fought all around the world taken into consideration, it is quite possible to tell that the world is passing through a massive crisis roots which go back to the formation of the civilizations. This chapter explores the differences in the genetic codes of the eastern and western civilizations' approach to the existing and potential conflicts by highlighting the role of religious, ethnic and sectarian factors in addition to the impact of ignorance on the conflict prevention process. It also offers solid public diplomacy solutions for bringing the conflicted communities together by reinterpreting the lessons learned from history of civilizations.

Keywords: Conflicts, Terrorism, Public Diplomacy, Civilizations

Dear President and representatives of Global Public Diplomacy Network, I welcome you all to Istanbul, the historical capital of two great civilizations and the meeting point of the great civilizations of our world, and I hope that this project brings goodness to humanity. Esteemed guests – we live in the very bosom where the heart of history beats.

"Sultanahmet Square,"[1] is a place where the incidents of two great civilizations, Byzantine (Eastern Roman) and Ottoman empires, took place. Not far from here rest the Hagia Sophia and Topkapı Palace, which stand as living examples of how history has taken shape and which have witnessed conflicting and unifying approaches.

---

1 The international conference which brought together academics, diplomats, bureaucrats, public and cultural diplomacy experts as well as students from and around the world is held in the hearth of Historical Peninsula which is called Sultan Ahmet, believed to be the meeting point of the civilizations for more than 8500 years.

Just 200 meters from here you can see a stone built in Eastern Rome. Back then, that stone which is known as "Million Stone,"[2] was the center of the earth and all roads spanned from that point across the world. You can see it on the other side of the square. If you walk a bit further, you'll see Süleymaniye Mosque. Upon entering the courtyard of the mosque, built by Sultan Suleiman the Magnificent, you see a pattern on marble – this is the sun disk, a symbol that Süleymaniye was the center of the earth. The Roman Empire. The Ottoman Empire. Christianity. Islam. As two civilizations that served as defining forces for shaping our world, each tried to understand the world in their own ways.

To understand these roots, let us together take a journey into history – I'd like to begin there as we are all a part of it.

Further down, we see the Hagia Sophia Mosque, the church of "Holy Wisdom." The day after he conquered Istanbul, Sultan Mehmed the Conqueror visited this church of Holy Wisdom and prayed there. Later on, he called out to the people of the city, who were Christian citizens of the Eastern Roman Empire, and made a speech saying, "You are free. You will continue to live in your own country, free to perform your traditions, customs and religious rituals. Free to choose your leaders."[3] Right then and there, he asked those people who were cast into a great war what they wanted and strived to meet their demands. Meanwhile, he was accompanied by Gennadius II, who would become the Ecumenical Patriarch of Constantinople. Gennadius had great knowledge and a scholarly demeanor. He was well-versed in the works of Aristotle and Ibn Rushd. He reminded the people of Byzantium one thing. When the Ottomans, Turks, came to conquer Istanbul, a Roman delegation was here. The delegation said, "You convert from Orthodox to Catholic and we'll save you from

---

2   The Million Stone, which is located very close to the entrance of the Hagia Sophia, is regarded as the "Zero Point," where the Roman Empire started, and the distances from and to Roman Empire were measured in accordance with that point.

3   It is known that Fatih Sultan Mehmet (Sultan Mehmet the Conqueror) provided many privileges to the Christian citizens of the former Eastern Roman Empire, protecting their social, cultural, ethnic and religious identities through his first executive order right after the conquest of the city of Istanbul. It is also believed that the approach displayed by Fatih Sultan Mehmet illustrates the Sultan's attitude as well as his stance toward cultural diversity and human rights.

the Ottomans, Turks." The Roman delegate, who was still present during the siege, told them to convert. Gennadius retreated to his rooms and said, "We cannot leave the religion of our ancestors. We should fight back no matter what." Sultan Mehmed made the man, who advised the people to fight back against Ottomans, the patriarch.

The same sultan would gather scholars from all across the world and engage in deep conversation with them at the pavilion of Topkapı Palace, which I think you'll visit soon. He also invited another scholar of trained in the traditions of St. Thomas and Aristotle, an Istanbulite religious scholar, from Rome and asked him to translate texts from Christian philosophy, including St. Thomas, into Arabic. He had the astronomical book of Ptolemy translated and also invited famous painter Bellini to make his portrait.

All of these were historical events, but let's remember that roots of history lie at the core of conflicts, disagreements, divisions and mutual animosity. If we don't interpret these roots correctly - or misread them - then history starts throwing rocks at us. Those incidents turn into stones cast upon us.

roots of history lie at the core of conflicts, disagreements, divisions and mutual animosity. If we don't interpret these roots correctly - or misread them - then history starts throwing rocks at us. Those incidents turn into stones cast upon us.

The primary reason that Mehmed the Conqueror and Gennadius acted in accordance with not each other but aligned values lies in the name of Hagia Sophia – Holy Wisdom, Saint Sophia, "sophos," i.e. wisdom.

Wisdom is an important concept for Muslims. It is mentioned in the Quran 17 times: "Wisdom is the greatest blessing Allah gave to humans. He gives it to whomever He wishes along with goodness." So, "Wisdom is the foundation of all goodness." The Prophet Muhammad, peace be upon him, also elevated wisdom: "Wisdom is the lost property of humanity; you should take it whenever you find it. Wisdom has no religion, culture or nation; everything that is true should be taken."

There were some who told Sultan Mehmed Conqueror to demolish Hagia Sophia out of revenge. Some even offered to cast out all Christians out of the country to Sultan Selim I, Sultan Mehmed Conqueror's grandson. When the Spaniards took control of Granada and forced all Jews and Christians to go on exile, the notables of the period told again to Sultan Selim I, to "cast out Christians in return". The Sultan Selim I, asked the Shaykh Al-Islam Zembilli Ali Efendi if this was the right thing to do, and he replied that, "This is against our belief. It cannot happen. We cannot blame someone for someone else's crimes." And since then, people from over 20 races, talking more than 20 languages and with more than 20 different beliefs in the Ottoman Empire found out the inconceivable secret of living together peacefully. Unfortunately, in the 21st-century, highly digitalized communication age, we still haven't managed to attain this peacefulness, and this, we might say intelligently, is the root of all our problems.

All prominent scholars of our time agree that the world is going through a big crisis which is based on civilization – we are passing through a civilizational crisis at the heart of which lies zealotry, ignorance, intolerance, prejudice, animosity, grudges and hate - which turn into acts of violence and terror, spreading bloody wars and embolden a tendency toward violence all around. This places us in an inextricable situation. We are paying great prices for this crisis in terms of history! We don't have to go too far to see this. Besides the people who were killed in Syria and millions of people exiled, the country lost its historical heritage of 5,000 years. They bombed and demolished the Great Mosques of Damascus and Aleppo. The latter was built as a pagan sanctuary 5,000 years ago. Then, it turned into a Roman sanctuary, and was then used for centuries as a Christian church. When the Muslims conquered the region, they used those sacred spaces as a church and a mosque. For 70 years, Muslims and Christians used the sanctuary together. It was one of the continuously used sanctuaries in the history, but a group who claimed to believe in the same religion demolished this history of 5,000 years without any hesitation. Nothing can be a greater calamity, because this is the destruction of civilization.

When Baghdad was invaded and attacked, historical heritage of 7,000 years was destroyed. However, as the Professor Nacos perfectly expressed, this terrible loss was mentioned either little or not at all in the press. (But a Hollywood star can take up an entire page or all TV channels.)

The crisis that we are facing threatens the essence of the global values that humanity has created over the centuries. Our planet has become uninhabitable due to the pollution and erosion of humanitarian and moral values; social, cultural and economic imbalances between countries in addition to war; conflicts and terrorism. These conflicts and imbalances are mostly based on religious, ethnic or sectarian reasons; however, no solution seems realistic and rational enough to solve these problems. What we have are radical solutions that breed new areas of conflict, deepening our inability to solve the ones we currently face.

conflicts and imbalances are mostly based on religious, ethnic or sectarian reasons; however, no solution seems realistic and rational enough to solve these problems. What we have are radical solutions that breed new areas of conflict, deepening our inability to solve the ones we currently face.

Ignorance or misinformation feeds fanaticism which leads to terror. The situation becomes even more complicated, especially when the ignorance is about religion. People who are ignorant about their own beliefs cannot healthily correlate between the values they believe in and the lives they are living, and thus fail to adapt. In such a case, they either distance themselves from life and display irrational behaviors which end in terrorism or belittle their values and become alienated with their cultures and identities.

Ignorance by all means play a very crucial role in global conflicts. Ignorance or misinformation feeds fanaticism which leads to terror. The situation becomes even more complicated, especially when the ignorance is about religion. People who are ignorant about their own beliefs cannot healthily correlate between the values they believe in and the lives they are living, and thus fail to adapt. In such a case, they either distance themselves from life and display irrational behaviors which end in terrorism or belittle their values and become alienated with their cultures and identities.

There is a highly common misconception in the public opinion that the current conflicts that we face today and the potential solutions offered to those conflicts are managed from the same spot by yet unidentified authorities. This really damages the trust put in the "five great nations," as it is mentioned by Turkey many times, "the world is bigger than five" who are the superpowers that administer international organizations, primarily the United Nations. Today, the world no longer trusts these privileged five powers of the United Nations. The incidents happening especially in the Middle East stand as an explicit proof of this.

Therefore, suggestions for solving conflicts often turn into factors that support this lack of solution in the first place. This concept is further visible

There is a highly common misconception in the public opinion that the current conflicts that we face today and the potential solutions offered to those conflicts are managed from the same spot by yet unidentified authorities. Today, the world no longer trusts these privileged five powers of the United Nations. The incidents happening especially in the Middle East stand as an explicit proof of this.

especially when it comes to conflicts about the Middle East and Islam. Considering the structure and development processes of terrorist organizations and their actions, we see that they are conducting ambiguous acts that conflict or outright contrast with their declared beliefs, which causes a difference of perception.

The violent incidents in the Islamic world are the acts of terrorism for the West. However, some people in the Islamic world are unfortunately taking these incidents as self-defense, which empowers terrorism. There's a very simple way to prevent this; openness, transparency, fairness and conscience can easily solve all this. Frequently seen both in global terrorist organizations such as Al-Qaeda, and in regional and national terrorist groups such as Daesh and Boko Haram, their declared goals and actions definitely contradict each other. I'll just give on example. The Holy Quran explicitly says that "If one intentionally kills a person, then he kills entire humanity."

Now, if Daesh and Al-Qaeda, who claim to be believer of a religion which affirms the statement which I have just quoted, put a knife on someone's throat and kill them in order to achieve their goals, neither myself nor any innocent believer of Islam would believe in them. Unfortunately, international organizations define this as Islamic terrorism rather than pointing out this aspect of the problem.

On the other hand, we also see that most international organization, NGOs and governmental organizations make non-objective evaluations. Moreover, we witness them ignore the areas where they should intervene. In most cases when they can intervene, they ignore

The heartbreaking incidents in Palestine, Kashmir, Cyprus, Bosnia, Azerbaijan Karabakh, Afghanistan, Iraq, Libya, Syria, Africa, and more recently in Myanmar, both feed the sense of hate felt by Muslims and continue to be a dark stain on the face of humanity. In order to overcome these issues, global powers should immediately take action, and act according to values of fairness, justice and humanity.

it and provide a ground for the process to continue. It creates an atmosphere of chaos in the international scene. The heartbreaking incidents in Palestine, Kashmir, Cyprus, Bosnia, Azerbaijan Karabakh, Afghanistan, Iraq, Libya, Syria, Africa, and more recently in Myanmar, both feed the sense of hate felt by Muslims and continue to be a dark stain on the face of humanity. In order to overcome these issues, global powers should immediately take action, and act according to values of fairness, justice and humanity.

I've tried to explain that most of the current conflicts are based on past conflicts and historical contexts. Now, it's high time to start a movement of the "virtuous" who will stop these negative developments, will put humanitarian values above all else, and will advocate for the righteous and fight against injustice. It has become an obligation to shake ourselves anew with a new birth, broaden our intellectual horizon, expand our perspective, enrich our spirituality, and work to spread a new understanding of civilization in all societies. This is one of the most important duties history has put on our shoulders. With this mindset, the Alliance of Civilizations was initiated in 2005 as part of the United Nations with the leadership of Recep Tayyip Erdoğan and José Luis Rodríguez Zapatero of Spain. This initiative currently comprises 128 countries and 28 international organizations. However, as I said earlier, the greater communities which come together to decide our fates carry multiple conflict of interest, and often act lazy or even reluctant when it comes to cultural and civilizational acts that will decide the destiny of humanity.

The Alliance of Civilizations is one of the most useful elements in terms of conflict resolution and the goals of public diplomacy. To this end, the Alliance of Civilizations Turkey prepared a 20-episode documentary, each 45-minute long, that portrays the 12,000-year-long history of civilizations and resembles a "River Flowing West." We have tried to portray a common history of civilizations from 9000 BC to AD 2010, the date when the Alliance of Civilizations was founded. We interviewed over 200 notable scholars for this project. We also prepared an international version of this documentary. It's a 7-hour-long documentary of civilization. It's been broadcasted on 43 TV channels around the world and reached millions of people.

Just as we were expecting to benefit from this documentary, ISIS came about and spread those images of world-threatening calamity. Since then, the broadcast of the documentary has come down to minimum; it's maybe on a few channels at most. This is about misinformation and misrepresentation.

This way, I personally experience this phenomenon because they represent Islam as a religion of sword, violence and murder.

The Alliance plays multiple beneficial roles in our society. In addition to these documentaries, we organize many events, but I don't want to go into details and take up too much of your time. I'd like to emphasize just one - the Institute of Alliance of Civilizations in Istanbul. The institute provides master's and doctoral education. We accept 20 students every year; half of them are Turkish and half are foreigners. Currently, 100 students from countries like China, Japan, the US and Brazil are receiving their master's and doctorate degrees at the institute.

The institute provides education in four languages: Turkish, English, Arabic and Spanish. The aim of the institute is to build a concept of civilization based on scientific, academic and intellectual knowledge. There are students from 40 countries speaking 8–10 different languages studying at the institute. In Istanbul, the heart of civilizations, we raise a young generation that embraces all civilizations as global values and accepts that each has its own internal values and that these should be advocated for.

Conflict resolution is very important, but we have to build this on firm grounds, and unite to mend the wrong aspects. As I said, wisdom is very important to us. Since I have a background in philosophy, I can talk about it for hours and days, but I'd like to end our discussion with a couplet. All this mysterious, philosophical and intellectual accumulation was summarized in two lines by Yunus Emre, who lends his name to our institute: "Love the created. For the Creator's sake." Unless we embrace all of humanity, accept everyone as brothers and sisters, and work to elevate, improve and cultivate people instead of destroying them, we will not be able to save ourselves from these misfortunes.

> *"Love the created. For the Creator's sake." Unless we embrace all of humanity, accept everyone as brothers and sisters, and work to elevate, improve and cultivate people instead of destroying them, we will not be able to save ourselves from these misfortunes.*

And I repeat, we must build a new sense of civilization in all societies because it is the only way to identify and address our multitude of challenges. I'd like to offer my congratulations to the President for bringing such a rare community together in a historical location like Istanbul where we'll surely find some feasible solutions. Thank you for your attention and kind consideration of our ideas.

Luan Starova, Macedonian Academy of Sciences and Arts

Luan Starova

Macedonian Academy of Sciences and Arts

Chapter 4
Cultural Diplomacy for Humanity's Common Benefit

Abstract: Building bridges between people of diverse and conflicting cultures can only be achieved by through special efforts of public and cultural diplomats who are particularly educated and trained for this mission. This mission is thought to be highly difficult in the regions like Balkans where there are so many conflictual factors for tearing the people from each other even in the same city. These factors include, but not limited to, the social, cultural, ethnic, religious, lingual, political, motivational, geographic differences and diversities as in the case of Balkans. This chapter investigates the role of public diplomacy in bringing conflicted communities by associating the best practices applied by Ottoman Empire for keeping the peoples of Balkans living in harmony.

Keywords: Public Diplomacy, Balkans, Conflicts, Ottoman Empire, Cultural Diversities

As an author registered to Macedonian Academy of Sciences and Arts based in Skopje and a former diplomat, I was truly impressed when I was invited to attend this international conference hosted by Yunus Emre Institute Cultural Diplomacy Academy and Global Public Diplomacy Network (GPDNet). I have so many interlinked reasons to accept this invitation, and I'd like to share them with you because of their importance. There are more pressing matters that I would like to emphasize on the "Cultural Diplomacy for Humanity's Common Benefit." In other words, the main reason I have accepted this invitation to attend this exquisite international conference is that I have wanted to highlight the real mission undertaken by cultural diplomacy to spread tangible and intangible values of civilization in the collective memory of humanity in the age of globalization. In this age we are experiencing, the effects of technological advancement paradigms spread quickly while simultaneously and frequently conflicting with the values of civilization we have in common.

In this period of time, when the digital civilization's characteristic values are on the rise and media revolutions occur, classical diplomacy is facing new generation challenges that it has never encountered before. This situation is especially seen when a body of civilization imposes its values on another one. As a citizen of the Republic of Macedonia in the heart of Southeast Europe, a small country that bears in its culture traces of many empires from ancient Greek and Roman civilizations to the Byzantine, Slovenian civilizations to the Ottomans for more than 20 centuries, I can present Macedonia as an example in terms of realizing public diplomacy goals on a national, international and long-term universal scale.

Looking at history in general and its major players in particular, it can be seen that the history of empires who focused on expansion and re-drawing of their borders through wars and invasions falls shorter than the cultural values inherited from the former civilizations, which were discarded into the background, but have managed to be kept alive by being passed from one generation to the next. Unfortunately, the creators of glorious victories in the book of history were unable to value these priceless cultural and humanitarian values in addition to shared richness of diversity.

> *history of empires who focused on expansion and re-drawing of their borders through wars and invasions falls shorter than the cultural values inherited from the former civilizations, which were discarded into the background, but have managed to be kept alive by being passed from one generation to the next.*

Considering this past heritage (which is not such a source of pride) left to us in terms of priceless shared cultural and humanitarian values, common richness of differences, the fundamental mission of "public and cultural diplomacy" today is to establish a harmony between differences by emphasizing cultural and humanitarian values that feed on the same or similar roots in this global mentality.

> *fundamental mission of "public and cultural diplomacy" today is to establish a harmony between differences by emphasizing cultural and humanitarian values that feed on the same or similar roots in this global mentality.*

I believe that as a human and an author, and as a member of a Muslim family living in a region between Albania and Macedonia whose roots date back to the Ottoman rule in the Balkans, I have been supporting this process by using instruments of literature and history. As the author of a romantic Balkan epic, writing 20 novels that reveal differences of the 20th Century and the people of that century, and enable new generations to meet on common ground around these differences.

In my literary works, I focus on the 500-year-long Ottoman rule in the Balkan Peninsula, especially the period when the rule of the Ottoman Empire ended in Albania and Macedonia, and the intentions and actions of the Western powers that collaborated with the nation-states born from the nationalities of the period. I strive to portray the synthesis of Ottoman and Islamic civilization that Western powers left between a vague life and a certain death and wished to exterminate and destroy along with its symbols for five centuries, and a period of multidimensional and keen settlement they participated in with this civilization's innocent representatives or victims. Actually, this is no different than what the aforementioned glorious victors of the history wished to achieve. What remains alive despite all these malicious intentions is the shared humanitarian and cultural values that have been created for centuries in spite of some physical differences and will be passed onto the new generations.

Through public and cultural diplomacy, it's possible to attain important achievements in the Balkans, which is home to many cultural diversities. However, to achieve this goal, one should reject the political attitude (and similar prejudices) that aim at the innocent Turkish and Ottoman communities to eliminate the tolerance, mutual trust and common values between Muslim and Christian communities in the period that began with the fall of the Ottoman Empire and continued throughout the 20th Century. Unfortunately, though it's been more than a century since the fall of the Ottoman Empire, the prejudices of the past have been kept alive by being passed down from one generation to the next. To our regret, we observed this in the Yugoslavian civil war in addition to the tragedies in Bosnia and Kosovo. As a result of past grudges of nationalistic powers, innocent people in many corners of the Balkans, as in Srebrenica, paid the price of their differences with their lives.

Germany and France, which conducted a type of war rarely seen in the past and experienced many casualties, not only formed a closer relationship despite their past animosity, but also raised their younger generations with historical research and tragedies and managed to write a shared history that displayed ways of economic growth. Unfortunately,

> *Germany and France, which conducted a type of war rarely seen in the past and experienced many casualties, not only formed a closer relationship despite their past animosity, but also raised their younger generations with historical research and tragedies and managed to write a shared history that displayed ways of economic growth.*

it's not possible to say the same about the long-established conflicts between states which were formed within the Ottoman nationalist system and lived under the shadow of the Western empires in the Balkans. That's why, I believe that the realization of such a project, which bears importance in terms of both Balkan countries and the Republic of Turkey's integration to the United Nations, by the Global Public Diplomacy Network will greatly contribute to regional peace and the unification of polarized communities in the European Union.

During the Ottoman reign in the Balkans (especially between the 14th and 20th centuries) Islamic values in language, culture, art and other spiritual areas became a part of the identity of Balkan people. The most drastic language features of the Balkans developed during the reign of the Ottoman Empire. This is an outcome of centuries-long communication and interaction of language, and this process resulted in a ceaseless convergence of various languages, known as "unity of Balkan languages." In simpler terms, it means that you cannot learn someone else's language just by going to school; you also have to learn it in their "neighborhoods." In his work "Tower of Babel" French philosopher Jacques Derrida says that "every language can atrophy through solitude and isolation, that every language evokes another language, but that the development of languages is also possible through mutual interaction." Though this information is part of a wider historical and theoretical picture, mutual interaction begins with becoming familiar with language and culture. In this regard, the valuable efforts to bring together differences by the Republic of Turkey's Yunus Emre Institute Culture Centers - that operate in Macedonia, other Balkan countries and many other corners of the world, and is named after great poet and mystic Yunus Emre, who wrote his works in Turkish, the language of the people, was a part of Anatolian wisdom, and known for his works Divan and Risaletü'n Nushiyye - are evidently exemplary steps in public diplomacy and cultural diplomacy. Bearing the traces of the amicable interaction between Bektashi, Mawlawi and Yasawi orders, Yunus Emre was a true mystic and a master of Turkish language. Through these culture centers, he will not only become one of the most admired poets in Turkey and a wider geography, but also become a symbol of unity of people from different religions, languages and cultures. Rumi, who was a contemporary and fellow scholar of Yunus Emre and lived the way of the dervish Anatolia, learned ancient Greek to bring Muslims and Christians together, and is therefore a great example that learning a language is the only way to interaction between and understanding differences.

Notable French philosopher Edgar Morin says that "two incidents bear great importance in the creation of the Mediterranean identity." According to Morin, "the first incident was the Andalusian experience which derived from the peaceful coexistence of three religions (Islam, Catholicism and Judaism) in Cordoba, and the second one was Rumi's effort to seek ways to make peace between Islam and Christianity by learning ancient Greek."

If we were to dig deeper, Arabs arrived the Iberian Peninsula in 711, and Islamic reign on the peninsula reached its peak in the 10th century. This climate of tolerance in Andalusia, which continued into the 12th century, a period that witnessed the life of Ibn Rushd (known as Averroes in Europe for his interpretations of Aristotle's philosophical and other texts), continues to remain a mysterious period for more than 800 years.

In later periods, one can find a similar time of tolerance in nearby geographies. As you may know, Sultan Bayezid II welcomed the Jewish people with no additional conditions when they were banished from Spain and Portugal by King of Spain Ferdinand in 1542. This doubtlessly poses a gesture of tolerance in extraordinary historical circumstances because during that period no state would take such a step for an exiled community while the Ottoman Empire proved their tolerance. Sultan Bayezid II's gesture can be traced back to the sayings of Prophet Muhammad "The difference between people are a blessing from God."

Sultan Bayezid II welcomed the Jewish people with no additional conditions when they were banished from Spain and Portugal by King of Spain Ferdinand in 1542. This doubtlessly poses a gesture of tolerance in extraordinary historical circumstances because during that period no state would take such a step for an exiled community while the Ottoman Empire proved their tolerance.

Finally, I'd like to say that with its social, cultural, artistic and educational activities in many parts of the world, primarily in Macedonia and in the Balkans, Yunus Emre Institute's culture centers have done and continue to do a successful job in improving its rich heritage of tolerance and co-existence and passing this down to next generations. The philosophy and power that feeds this precious heritage, and the collection of knowledge based on justice and equity can be regarded as the safest assurances of bringing together conflicting communities and their differences via public and cultural diplomacy.

Luis Palma Castillo, Ministry of National Defense of Chile

Luis Palma Castillo

Ministry of National Defense of Chile

Chapter 5
Social Media in Public Diplomacy as a Leverage to Traditional Diplomacy

Abstract: The history of cross cultural interactions can be taken far back to the prehistoric times in terms, but 1980s should be taken as a mile stone for the start of globalization. The advances in Internet as well as in Computer and Information Technologies also accelerated the rate of the cross-cultural communication and created networked communities. Today, governments need to engage with the foreign public more than ever through their foreign services in order to secure their national and collective interests. This chapter scrutinizes the role of social media in public diplomacy, while questioning whether the public diplomacy efforts should be led by traditional diplomats or by NGOs through the contributions and the guidance of public diplomacy experts.

Keywords: Globalization, Diplomacy, Public Diplomacy, National Interests, Collective Interests, Social Media

Though the history of interactions between cultures and civilizations can be traced back to prehistoric times in terms of commercial relationships, it would be a smart choice to take the '80s as a reference point as the beginning of globalization in the modern sense. In addition to incidents that occurred after 1980 such as the fall of the Berlin Wall, the USSR and the Eastern bloc, the increasing number of multinational companies brought societies closer than ever in the social sense thanks to the technical advancements in technology, transportation and communication.

First, if we are to examine this process via news production and distribution channels and media tools, we can see some drastic changes regarding the information and communication technologies in the working dynamics of media organizations such as BBC, CNN, EURONEWS and Al-Jazeera, which has recently and strikingly entered our lives that send journalists to all corners of the world, build stations and collect news to understand and relay what happens in this old planet of ours. Here, the role of information and communication technologies and the Internet is considerably big in unifying the masses in a multifaceted way. Today, people who have *the role of information and communication technologies and the Internet is considerably big in unifying the masses in a multifaceted way. Today, people who have access to the Internet have the opportunity to ceaselessly communicate with each other via social platforms*

access to the Internet have the opportunity to ceaselessly communicate with each other via social platforms such as Twitter, YouTube, Instagram and Facebook (which has more than 1.4 billion users), share their moments, and can follow changes in real time. In addition to bringing people together and helping them to form friendship groups around these social networks, these communication platforms also enable people to share with the world the social, cultural, economic and political developments in their social circles, and to gain awareness by learning about what's going on around the world right from the source.

Another incident that gave birth to the concept of social network, which is the new form of communication and interaction between masses, is the wind of Arab Spring that fiercely blew for a period in the Middle East and northern part of Africa. The fact that the young Egyptians, who received messages on their cell phones to mobilize and participate in the protests to overthrow the Hosni Mubarak regime in Egypt, gathered around the Tahrir Square in Egypt is a very impressive example in terms of the influence of social networks. At the heart of the fall of the Hosni Mubarak regime lies the influence of the messages spread via various social media platforms and cell phones on the younger population. One should keep in mind that as a result of the negative influence in Egypt which resulted from the protesting masses under the effect of social media platforms, the military took control and ended the Hosni Mubarak regime.

Considering social networks' power and influence to gather masses in different geographical and intellectual ecosystems and to immobilize them around common goals, the use of these new tools of communication become well-regarded in raising national and international awareness about any kind of issue in terms of social, cultural, economic and political priorities. It should not be forgotten that public and mass behavior analyses on social media would provide you with the

It should not be forgotten that public and mass behavior analyses on social media would provide you with the determining factors for the position you'll take as a country about the incidents in any part of the world in a detailed manner.

determining factors for the position you'll take as a country about the incidents in any part of the world in a detailed manner.

Looking at the topic of public diplomacy from an international relations aspect, Bruce Gregory explains this US-based concept which enables creating awareness against global problems in the targeted mass as follows:

> public diplomacy has come to mean an instrument used by states, associations of states, and some sub-states and non-states actors to understand cultures, attitudes and behavior; to build and manage relationships; and to influence thoughts and mobilize actions to advance their interests and values.[1]

It's possible to present many special cases that confirm this concept defined by Bruce Gregory in broad strokes. Firstly, looking at the negative use of public diplomacy, the first actor is doubtless Julian Assange, who put the United States of America in an impossible position against its allies with "Wikileaks," by spreading thousands of confidential US documents on the Internet. Another example would be Edward Snowden, a CIA (Central Intelligence Agency) who had to apply for an asylum in the Russian Federation for leaking confidential US documents like Assange did, and is still living there. With their leaks, Assange and Snowden dealt a blow to the realization of USA's national and international interests and created a worldwide negative perception.

Considering the influence of social media shares on public diplomacy, what also requires attention is to share fragile information and documents via confirmed communication networks. The world still hasn't forgot about the negative image the former US Secretary of State and presidential nominee Hillary Clinton created in the national public opinion by using her personal email account instead of the official and secure communication account of the Department of State.

Let's take Catalonia as an example to talk about the use of social media platforms to raise awareness in the international scene in terms of the struggle for independence in relation to public diplomacy - in order to prevent the mobilization of those who support independence in the last referendum, the Madrid government prevented access to the referendum website used by the Barcelona government. Carles Puigdemont, who was the president then, opened two new websites in London via his own Twitter account. By acting

---

1 Gregory, Bruce. *American Public Diplomacy: Ending characteristics, Elusive transformation*. The Hague Journal of Diplomacy, Special Issue on US Diplomacy, (forthcoming 2011) page. 3.

as such, Puigdemont prevented the officials of the Madrid government to shut down their website, continues to promote himself to the Catalans and to the world about the goals and purposes of the referendum in general, and succeeded in bringing more supporters to the government-led movement.

I believe that us diplomats, who are the operators of traditional diplomacy, have to behave in a very careful and tempered manner in terms of using public diplomacy. We should keep in mind that – in most cases – people with access to these types of communication and interaction platforms believe that it is their right and freedom to express their thoughts and ideas without being equipped with the necessary amount of knowledge in social, cultural, economic, political and intra-state relations that regard them in a direct or indirect way. It is also known that certain irresponsible shares on social networks by organizations and establishments such as think tanks, NGOs, universities, media and research centers that require a sensitivity about and knowledge for traditional diplomacy can also jeopardize the relationships between countries.

Looking at the potential danger of such shares with problematic or irresponsible content on social media platforms, the first threat is that these types of content can quickly spread around social media platforms. A second, and more important, threat is the possibility for that problematic and irresponsible content to create an unwanted influence on the public opinion, and that it can be used by third parties to cause irredeemable harm to mutual interests through misinformation and even manipulation.

The use of public diplomacy by qualified diplomats who are well-versed in the balances and priorities of traditional diplomacy as a method and a strategy will doubtlessly contribute to the improvement of international relations.

The use of public diplomacy by qualified diplomats who are well-versed in the balances and priorities of traditional diplomacy as a method and a strategy will doubtlessly contribute to the improvement of international relations. Public diplomacy, which enables ceaseless interaction via social networks, is no doubt a useful and fast tool. In this regard, governments can gain support that requires the public's attention for rightful and prioritized reasons and can develop effective crisis management policies in a short amount of time. Moreover, by utilizing traditional diplomacy teachings on social networks, it's possible to use this method with public support to condemn, deny or refute an incident.

Of course, traditional diplomacy should benefit from the advantages of social media platforms that deem public diplomacy fast and flexible; however, it would definitely be right to take the flow of information and shares by official sources as a reference to understand, listen to and evaluate what people think about an incident. Otherwise, in cases where we are not sure about the credibility of news from the unofficial source, official channels should never respond before confirming the received information. Though today many people criticize "old-school" diplomacy for its slow and heavy procedures, this new form of diplomacy will not change the old one. Classical diplomacy requires a depth of experience, great knowledge and patience to reach its goals. As is known, negotiation is the most frequently used tool in diplomacy, and it necessitates time, experience, knowledge and command.

Without question, the thoughts, tendencies and reactions of the people who are regarded as the target audience in public diplomacy about social, cultural and economic regulations can be used as signifiers in that they provide an analytical opinion about understanding the public opinion, and what people are interested in and what they say about it, i.e. "word on the street." In case of carrying out public diplomacy via social media tools, it is of vital importance to measure its influence on the public opinion. Thanks to content analysis tools that require advanced technology, it's now possible to keep track of the public opinion and to understand the change of behavior in the target audience. Therefore, the feedback of the target audience via social media for public diplomacy is very important and valuable in correctly evaluating whether the public is for or against an incident/development.

Well-managed and properly utilized, public diplomacy can be a perfect tool to support traditional diplomacy in realizing national and collective interests. Considering its feasibility to collaborate with traditional diplomacy in turning to public support to give direction to endless negotiations and to end potential conflicts, public diplomacy should be regarded as a vital force multiplier that increases the effectiveness of traditional diplomacy.

Part Two

PANEL DISCUSSION

The Future and the Role of Public Diplomacy in Conflict Prevention

Moderator:
Melih Barut | Yunus Emre Institute Cultural Diplomacy Academy

Panelists:
Brigitte L. Nacos | Columbia University
Bekir Karlığa | United Nations Alliance of Civilizations National
                           Coordination Committee
Luis Palma | Ministry of National Defense of Chile

Melih Barut

Yunus Emre Institute Cultural Diplomacy Academy

The Future of the Public Diplomacy and the Role of Public Diplomacy in Conflict Prevention

Abstract: Public diplomacy can be regarded as one of the most critical way of connecting state actors and their peoples to each other through organized efforts. These efforts can be defined as the diplomatic maneuvers conducted form governments to the foreign publics in order to bring the multidimensional differences together on a common ground and open space for the progress of traditional diplomacy through common social, cultural and universal humanitarian values. The world that we are living in today is passing through multi-reasoned as well as multilateral polarization process. Public diplomacy with its multidimensional tools is believed to be the best diplomatic practice that can be used long term in the conflict prevention process. This chapter puts forward notes of the panel entitled "The Future of the Public Diplomacy and the Role of Public Diplomacy in Conflict Prevention" and it also offers some valuable hand-on guidance to the public and cultural diplomats as well as to the strategic communication experts.

Keywords: Conflict Prevention, Diplomacy, Public Diplomacy, Civilizations, Cultural Diplomacy, Strategic Communication

The panel discussion on "The Future of the Public Diplomacy and the Role of Public Diplomacy in Conflict Prevention" is organized in cooperation with Yunus Emre Institute Cultural Diplomacy Academy and Global Public Diplomacy Network in order to explore how public and cultural diplomacy should be used in the field in conflict prevention process.

If we need to look at the reason behind why the subject of "The Future of the Public Diplomacy and the Role of Public Diplomacy in Conflict Prevention" is chosen for the panel discussion topic, when the raising political, social, cultural, religious, ethnopolitical and gender based polarizations in the world which from time to time reach to brutal violence taken into account, it is thought that discussing this topic would contribute both to the academic literature of public and cultural diplomacy as well as to the daily practices of the public and cultural diplomats in their field work.

The panel discussion is held right after the conference entitled "The Role of Public Diplomacy in Bringing Conflicted Communities Together". It is held with the valuable contributions of Professor Brigitte Nacos, Professor Bekir Karlığa and Ambassador Luis Palma. During the panel discussion, the various dimensions of the following questions are explored:

- How public and cultural diplomacy should be used in order to prevent conflicts in general and islamophobia in particular?
- How social and conventional media should be used in the process of conflict prevention and conflict resolution processes?
- How existing and potential polarizations reaching to violent conflicts between eastern and westerns civilizations should be resolved?
- Where exactly public and cultural diplomacy efforts should be located in practice, within or outside of the traditional diplomacy?
- How strategic communication as well as persuasion and influence activities should be associated with public diplomacy in order to solve the global conflictual problems peacefully?

PANEL DISCUSSION

MELİH BARUT: Professor Ateş, Presidency and representatives of esteemed Global Public Diplomacy Network members, candidate institutions, observers, distinguished guests, members of diplomatic leads in Turkey, and ladies and gentlemen.

In the morning session we have covered so many issues from different perspectives. Initially, we have planned all these happen in the form of panel discussion, but right now I would love to conduct this session in terms of open conversation, that would be better for exploring the unexplored dimensions of the subject that we are going to discuss.

Well, I guess most of you know our panelists already, but for the new comers, Professor Brigitte Nacos from Columbia University from the Department of Political Science, Professor Bekir Karlığa from Alliance of Civilization Initiative and finally Ambassador Luis Palma from the Ministry of National Defense of Chile.

In the last session, most of our colleagues are impressed with the presentations delivered by the distinguished speakers touching the different dimensions of the "The Role of the Public Diplomacy in Bringing Conflicted Communities Together". In this session we are going to discuss "The Future of the Public Diplomacy and the Role of Public Diplomacy in Conflict

Prevention." If I may, to warm up I would like to start with the teaser of the award-winning documentary named *The River Flowing Westward* by Dr. Bekir Karlığa, who has developed this documentary. During the break most of the questions that I was asked were mostly concentrated on the issue of Islamophobia, which has been a raising conflictual issue over the last two decades. As you know, the concentration of the panel is on "The Future of Public Diplomacy and the Role of Public Diplomacy in the Conflict Prevention." I want you to take the potential conflict here as Islamophobia. The question is: How we can use current tools – I mean communication, public diplomacy – in order to prevent this Islamophobia, happen and ruin all our lives? Okay, maybe we can start with Professor Nacos.

BRIGITTE L. NACOS: I think my college Professor Karlığa this morning said that these processes take time. So, you cannot accomplish something from today to tomorrow. I really think that the answer is education, and people to people exchanges. Because people have to first learn how to respect each other and they have to have knowledge. Islamophobia is based on ignorance and our professors this morning so well talked about the history of civilizations and how much cooperation between the regions was there. I think the answer is that we have to overcome this myth that it's a clash of civilization. I have spent a great deal of time to look at the communications after 9/11 between President Bush and people around him. And Bin Laden and other people high up in Al-Kaida. And basically, these were the same, both talked literally about the clash of civilizations. They basically said there's only one way and that is to destroy each other, one will win. Unfortunately, this still exists, I think all over the world. I know it particularly, of course, from the West, where I lived and I actually became a Western citizen. It is unbelievable what the far extremists spread about Islam. It is not at all based on reality. So how do you fight something like that? It has to be by documentaries like that, but you cannot force people to see it. One of the problem is today that there is a narrow passing of information, and that people do not look at a broad spectrum of information and knowledge, but rather look at something they agree with. So, if you do that you do not expand your horizon. The professor this morning, and I told him that's what I take home mostly and we expanded on this during lunch break. We have to have wisdom, people have to stop making quick judgments about religion. I think that's what one has to take if you come to that conclusion. I think that's really a charge of people who are active in public diplomacy. But I think that I'm not in an official function also, but I think when I teach I feel that it is my duty to tell the truth, to kind of make clear that at least my students, who understand a lot what they hear today, study and learn, and then go out and spread the word. So, there is no quick fix, but we cannot despair, we have to do something about it.

MELİH BARUT: Okay, Professor Karlığa, your opinions about the complicated problem? Well, actually, you are the mastermind on this issue and you have spent a lot of time constructing this award-winning documentary. So, you have touched the ground, you have talked with the people and so you have analyzed everything. And I guess you also know the ways of reaching to the new generations. So, your opinions?

BEKİR KARLIĞA: Dr. Barut, thank you very much for the very encouraging remarks. I hope that I would live up to your nice introduction. First of all, as I said before, inaccurate information, information pollution and some actions for the gain of certain interests are given away to all extremism, enmity spreading behaviors. Starting 9/11, Islamophobia started to rise among many people, but it didn't stop there. Certain terrorist trends emerged in our geography, even fired up the discussions around Islamophobia. In the second night of 9/11, I was in a panel to a news channel of Turkey, in NTV, I was also speaking on that program and my opinions have held the same ever since. This is not a project which can be perpetuated with the names which have been circulated in the media. There should be larger powers, there should be larger intentions behind this action. There was an American college in that talk, and he asked me: "Then, tell me who they are," and I said "wouldn't I tell if I knew," but what I knew is I know these people, I know, I'm an Eastern person, I was raised among the Eastern people. I know their capacity, I know their capabilities. It is not possible to come up with such an action with all this plain and complication, it was not possible to be done by these people. So, there is the invisible, I call them the "Evil Powers." There are some powers trying to orchestrate what we see here as an example of Islamophobia or the terrorist attacks. We don't see them, but we know who they are there. You cannot see the electricity, but you know it is there. You don't know about your death, but you know there is death. It is manipulated from one direction and they are trying to agitate some sensitivities of the society creating an artificial animosity and creating enemies towards each other. Islamophobia is a very open example of that. For 40 years I've been teaching the Eastern and Western comparative philosophies. And for all these 40 years I have thought that East and West have never been enemies to each other, but they are complimentary to each other because neither of them is full or complete without each other. However, there is a historical background behind all this. This historical background is constructed on inaccurate information from the very beginning and it starts with crusades. If you look carefully, in the emergence of crusades, the main understanding in the Western world back then was 'Islam is barbaric, pagan and Muslims are worshiping Hz. Muhammad and whenever they go to Mecca they worship and they are womanizers, Hz. Muhammad is womanizer etc. Where does this comes from? Juhannes Sames Senos in the 8th century, he is a Christian saint and lived in Damascus. At the beginning, he lived in the Ummayad Palace in Damascus. His father was the minister of economics, he was in charge of economics and finance, and he was a very influential person. But throughout the years he was less favored and he started to write some little booklets, 10-page, 8-page booklets. And since he was not happy with the situation, since he started to get against Islam, then he started to give inaccurate information about Islam. All these basics of crusades, all this inaccurate information is coming from his resources. All these ideas from the 8th century are the information foundations of the racists, chauvinist, Islamophobic understanding, demolishing the mosques, burning up the minarets, silencing the prayers. They share the exact same arguments. The clash between the East and the West, Christianity and Islam was born out of that. But in the 20th century, we came to a position where we can overcome all this inaccurate information, we can turn to a new page. But starting from after the collapse of the Soviet Union, as we discussed with Professor Neocon, and Evangelists, and these radical Christians; they also fueled such conflict. Some Buddhist movements, they want to get something out of this conflict. Therefore, they are trying to disseminate a conflict argument. But we should not put all the blame on the West, we should not put all the blame on Christianity, the same ignorance, same negligence is also quite common among Muslims. Whatever happens, they all take it as something against their religion and they react, they want to fight back. But this ignorance is causing a lot of pain, suffering for both nations, for both civilizations. Islamophobia, all terrorist activities, Turkophobia in the West, there is no rational basis. We were all together, we live all together in history and if we continue to be together, then the civilizations gain and we have all these enormous improvements in the history of human kind.

The only solution to all this is disseminating accurate information even if this accurate information is something against me, something that would devalue me, it should be disseminated. There is a huge role that needs to be played by the media. However, as the previous speakers mentioned, media is focusing on things which are quite abnormal, but the regular things, things that need to be heard, are not found interesting by the media and this is the common trend in all world media. Therefore, we need a mentality change, we need a change in our conception, our comprehension, and I think we should create a new awareness of civilization. If I have time in the forthcoming minutes, I'll give more details about this new awareness of civilizations.

MELİH BARUT: Ambassador Palma, if possible, I would like to take your comments from your dual academic and professional background. I mean, you are a historian, also you are a diplomat. How are diplomats situated in this context? What would be your suggestion?

LUIS PALMA CASTILLO: Well, first I want to let you know as a diplomat, I don't think that I have been any part of real politic school in thoughts on international relations. So, I have my own special point of view about this. First, conflicts are produced by global, regional and local interests. And the solution of these problems must be through negotiation and continuous communication. So, for me it's very important to have a good negotiation. I don't want to be alone in my speech, but I want to say negotiation is important for all of us. I was in Oslo negotiation process between Palestine and Israel. It was a great effort for both parties. I should admit that negotiation and communication process is really long and highly demanding and makes you take every single detail into consideration for mutual agreement. It is almost the same for the Syria case. As we all know, there is a great conflict of interests in Syria, many neighboring countries and non-neighboring countries. It is also a challenge of immediate interests and remote interests. Eventually, if we look at the picture from the humanitarian point of view, so many people are displaced, so many people including civilians lost their lives and so many children are traumatized because of the civil war in Syria. In this point, I believe that public diplomacy and cultural diplomacy would be a great tool for healing the wounds of traumatized people.

MELİH BARUT: Okay, thank you very much. In this session, we have almost answered the question. What I would like to know – maybe this question will go to Professor Nacos first since she comes from Political

Science and Journalism background – is: How can we use the media? How can we dominate or lead in the process of conflict resolution? What do you think? Is it possible in the context of social media as well?

BRIGITTE L. NACOS: Unfortunately, I think social media are used mostly for the negative and it is very difficult to do something about it. We have these issues right now; fake news is a big issue in the United States. Of course, the people who spread most fake news are the ones who fight against it in order to fight against the mainstream media. But now social media provide us, Twitter, Facebook, YouTube and others; they are supposed to kind of fight fake news, hate speech, incitement, but that creates a problem too. Because if you are going to put freedom of expression into the hand of private companies, you know… I fully agree that certain things shouldn't be on YouTube, like ISIS beheading people. Sometimes if you don't publish something, you kill something. Nevertheless, I have a great problem because where does it stop then? If you are going to put this great power to control freedom of expression into the hands of these private companies whose imperative is profit, it is a big problem, but these are the very vehicles to spread this kind of hate. Communication can be used for many things, it can be used in our context to unite people, but at the same time, it can bring people apart and very often that happens with the same messaging. I have to say again, back to the time after 9/11 when President Bush talked about the war on terrorism in one of his speeches. He united Americans who were scared, they had never seen this kind of an attack on the mainland, forget about Hawaii and Pearl Harbor. There was a real big shock there. So, people rallied behind the president. So, he united people. But the same message really did the opposite when it came to Arabs and Muslims and some others, because it divided people, it was a demagogic message that "it's we against them." So, that is the problem with communication. The mainstream media should be the one that at least try to find a good middle ground. But after the election of Mr. Trump, who is day in, day out contributing to the divide within and outside, there are people in the White House who think that Islamophobia is the scariest thing. The good news is that some of the leading mainstream media organizations like The New York Times, The Washington Post are the people who can do investigated reporting and they also can have educational effect because it happens in all countries. The major news organizations are leaders of the rest of the media. So that kind of message is then more spread. There have been many more resources that have gone into investigated reporting and reporting that would unite more. Both of these organizations have actually increased their circulation and even more so their online subscribers. So, all the news is not some good things about this.

MELİH BARUT: I just wanted you to give the example while we were talking, during the break time. You know media is intoxicating the upcoming generations as well. Video games, I mean.

BRIGITTE L. NACOS: No. That example was an example from Europe. You know, in the United States there is no law against hate speech, because this First Amendment simply does not allow to make laws. That's different in Europe. And I do have to say, as you can hear I have a German accent, in Austria, in Germany, in some other countries there are strict laws against hate speech. And that is, where else it was not followed through in the case of Danish cartoon issue, because Denmark has something like that too. In Austria, we have just seen a bad election and I don't know what's going to happen; they haven't formed a government. There was this case where they had – at first in Switzerland, then in Austria – an online video game, and the goal of that game was to shoot the minarets to prevent the call to prayers in these European countries. The people who put it up were immediately forced to take it back otherwise they would have been prosecuted and I'm very sure they would have been found guilty and would have been punished. I think there has to be something, there is a limit for what you can do, you know this sort of hate speech. I follow very strictly some of the extremist websites, Twitter and other accounts that are vilifying Islam and Muslims because I'm very concerned what happened to American Muslims. I think that's not only hate speech but also incitement. And I wish that some of the civil organizations would sue because there has been some press there, it has nothing to do with Islam, even in the United States.

MELİH BARUT: Thank you very much Professor Nacos for your valuable comments. Professor Karlığa, before I give the floor to you, I would like to turn and ask my question to Ambassador Palma coming all the way from Chile. Ambassador Palma, as I get back to your previous response, you mentioned that national interests or collective interests are the critical determiners for so many things in the international relations. So, I believe that there must be some other tools for reaching national and collective goals and objectives without creating any conflict at any level. I mean diplomatic means, economic means or coercive means for getting what you want through influence and persuasion. In this part, I would like to concentrate on the content of public diplomacy. What do you think: How should we implement persuasion and influence process to public diplomacy process to reach the goals and objectives peacefully? Your thoughts?

LUIS PALMA CASTILLO: We are living in a world composed of 194 countries. So, those are the solid actors of global political relations environment. So, diplomacy helps these actors communicate with each other. We have talked about the importance of communication in international system. Through diplomacy, states communicate bilaterally or multilaterally. Diplomacy is a professional track and must be done by the career people. Well, as for public diplomacy and cultural diplomacy, I believe that all these diplomatic processes must be conducted under the traditional diplomacy. In other words, the traditional diplomacy must orchestrate those tools. We don't separate them, but I think they must complement each other and must be under the traditional diplomacy.

MELİH BARUT: I guess there is an objection here. Professor Nacos.

BRIGITTE L. NACOS: Firstly, I would clearly have to distinguish between the classical government and government diplomacy and then public diplomacy. Public diplomacy is a form of diplomacy the governments or other organizations which are mostly funded by governments directly commutate and engage with the foreign public. That's basically what we talked about. And actually, this morning you quoted one of the British ambassadors who thinks an ambassador should Tweet more and communicate. I think that's very dangerous. It is very dangerous because that means an ambassador is to talk, you know, he is going to get into domestic policies; it actually happened with an American ambassador in Egypt, and if you remember there was a big problem there. No, traditional diplomacy is government to government, and I don't think any ambassador, whether in Germany, in the US, in Turkey or elsewhere, should really engage or maybe even divide factions within a country. I know that the last US ambassador in Moscow under Obama used to tweet or post on Facebook to introduce himself. Well that doesn't do any harm that people know who is sitting there, but don't get engaged. That's very different with public diplomacy and I think we must have a really good dividing line between them. And I think the best public diplomacy is designed and implemented not by governments directly, but by NGO's or other organizations. I believe that aid organizations for example show the greatest successes in changing catastrophes. The public opinion about Americans in Pakistan changed after the earthquake when the US military made tremendous efforts to help out the Pakistani People. The tsunami was another case.

MELİH BARUT: Thank you very much Professor Nacos for elaborating on the subject. Professor Karlığa, this is a turning in kind of like a discussion among ourselves and you were saying just recently that there is a need for a new perception of civilizations. Can you elaborate on that a little bit more?

BEKİR KARLIĞA: The most lasting concept that humanity has come up with is civilization. And people, humans who lose the understanding, perception of civilization, turn into barbarians. They kill their fathers, they kill their friends, they kill people around them. Yes, war always exists, I don't support it but it's a part of nature. Nevertheless, this doesn't mean that killing a human being is not a crime, it is the biggest crime of all. And our world over the last 300 years has also come up with the most magnificent successes it has ever achieved. The Western civilization has guided this lastly. But of course, the civilization has its own shortcomings and we see that historically. And fundamentally there is a lack of balance between logic, the mind and the heart. If you lose that balance, when a society can't balance that, then the societies lose their creativity. And westerners have it, but the Islamic world also has this problem and I can elaborate if you like; the Western world after the revolutions put the mind forward, they made the mind a priority and said that everything can be solved with the mind. Positivism, materialism and all of these "-isms" all focused on the mind and did not accept anything that could not be explained with the mind. And on the other hand, the Islamic world couldn't balance the mind and the heart, but this was a balance on the other hand. Between the 8th and the 12th Centuries, the Islamic world had its golden age. It was better than the Egyptian, the Indian and the Roman civilizations, and they came up with the Islamic civilization and its golden age, we elaborate on that in the documentary. However, as for the 16th century, when the Western civilization turned going up, the Islamic civilization gave up on the mind and they focused on the tradition. And that became a problem as well. And I think this is the fundamental problem of civilizations. The West focuses on the mind and the Islamic world just focuses on the belief, and the heart and the tradition. So, as for the 20th century, I think this was the fundamental factor shaping our world. Maybe this wasn't as important in the 18th and 19th Centuries as in the 1950's with technology, with communication and the vast development speed, it did not allow for this misbalance. The human race has to go back to its values, go back to thinking about itself, reevaluating and come up with a common denominator to rebuild a new perception. Let's not forget, for the last 300 years we have dwelled with civilization and as for the 18th century, this became an official concept in the Western civilization. Before civilization, back then it was only perceived as Western. It was like, the Westerners, wherever they went, they would take the civilization there because civilization didn't exist in the other part. And whatever civilization can mean, if you go somewhere, kill people and abolish everything that is there, what's the perception? The Eurocentric perception. We have to put that aside as well, and we have to rebuild a new civilization, perception. And we have the ability to do that, we have the conditions to do that, and that requires wisdom and we have that as well.

As to what role should Yunus Emre Institute and Global Public Diplomacy Network take over in order to contribute to the new perception of civilizations. I think these kind of gatherings, meetings, events should perpetuate and we have to get down to business, get down to the fundamentals. And we have to guide others who would like to follow in this path of perception, and we need concrete outputs. And I think it would be much more beneficial for the younger generations as well. Yes, we all have media problems. But on the other hand, we should not completely get rid of the media, we just need to guide them better because if you don't do something better than that means that something will only get worse. So, the GPDNet, the institute and others, we have to try and do our best. And that's how you can counterbalance the opposite part. And like the gentlemen and the lady were saying: "We have to be patient and patience will succeed." We have to pursue and we have to continue and we have to bring together these differences. And we have to create that alliance of civilizations. And that's what other third parties, actors should do as well. One example, in that documentary I did, in France 100 million people watched it within one day. I've been writing books for 50 years and I haven't been able to access 100 million people in 50 years, but I was able to do that overnight. So, I really realized the power of the media in that way. And we have to use that to enlighten our societies. Thank you very much and I think we have gotten our messages.

MELİH BARUT: Professor Karlığa, many thanks for the comments and guidance. I guess Ambassador Palma raised his hand earlier, so I have to turn to him. Please go ahead.

LUIS PALMA CASTILLO: We have heard about civilization in the West. I remember that somebody this morning said that Doctor Fujiyama was very happy when the cold war ended. The Soviet Union was defeated and the United States was also happy because democracy was the winner of competition at the end of the day. But we should not forget that democracy is a Western value. And I guess we cannot spread democracy to the world with arms and through military invasions.

BRIGITTE L. NACOS: I don't agree with Fujiyama, but I do have to say that he didn't say democracy and capitalism should be spread. He said that "it would be just naturally spreading" now for the rest of the world.

MELİH BARUT: Professor Karlığa, please.

BEKİR KARLIĞA: Now with the Ambassador's comment I can maybe say something else. Of course, democracy doesn't belong to the Western world, it's a universal value. Of course, making it belong to the Western world and thinking that other societies cannot achieve it is not true. And I think this is something that has been underlined in the Clash of Civilizations theory. In my own personal area of interest, maybe I can elaborate. One of the best writings on democracy belongs to Ibn Rüşd from the 13th–14th–15th Centuries and actually had an impact on European renaissance. Ibn Rüşd, known as Averroes, wrote a reference to Plato's laws and he said for democracy to be able to stand there was also a need for other values; and it was in 1180. And this is in our geography and in Spain, the Muslim Spain – the Andalusia, it was said that we tried and we weren't successful. So, actually, these values, these concepts, I don't think they should be made to belong to any civilization, any geography, any society. I think all societies have parts of these concepts. For example, the Quran, the holy book, describes decisions to be made through communes. And that's something that is a part of democracy today. So, the implementation was there, the Ottoman sultans, they didn't decide just by themselves. They had advisors, they had councils, communities, and that's how they decided. We pick and select these isolated incidents and we tend to comment on them without looking at their background. Therefore, I believe that we need to work on common values which can be shared by all humanity. These are actually evident both in the West and in the East, both in Christianity and Islam, and Confucianism and Hinduism. I think it wouldn't be a civilization if these concepts didn't exist anyway.

MELİH BARUT: Thank you very much for all your comments. Unfortunately, Professor Nacos here puts pressure on me to take some questions, and on the other hand the time is almost over. So, I really don't know how to manage it right now? Maybe we can get 1 or 2 questions from the audience. If there is any of course.

QUESTION (Mr. LUİS ERIOMALA – Nigeria): Good afternoon. The problem I would bring up is the radicalization among the youths. As you know Boko Haram is very active in Nigeria, mostly among the youths, and like Professor Karlığa said, it is because of the wrong education. What do you think: How can we solve this problem with the youths? Thank you.

MELİH BARUT: Professor Nacos, we can start with you. Please.

BRIGITTE L. NACOS: You know, I have spent the last 25 years studying terrorism and counterterrorism. Unfortunately, you cannot solve it peacefully. I do not believe in violence. But in some cases, I don't think you can solve the problem by education, by spreading the knowledge, you cannot solve that problem by negotiations. There are some people you cannot get to the table because they want to destroy the table and I think that's not the only case, there are some other cases like that. You basically have to do with a group who are against education and we know of course that the American special forces are helping those who don't know that. As I said, I don't like to say what I had to say, but I don't think there is a peaceful way out.

MELİH BARUT: Okay, thank you so much Professor Nacos. Professor Karlığa, please?

BEKİR KARLIĞA: In the Boko Haram case, yes, education cannot be enough by itself. Information, training and knowledge cannot be enough by itself, you have to change the environment, you have to correct the environment, socially, economically, politically, and without that you cannot be successful. And that country is unable to do it because of poverty. And that's why I'm focusing on this new perception of civilization. Then maybe we can shift the money we spend on wars to this kind of transformation. Then if you allow that kind of transformation, then people will be able to see a better truth. So, I think the international community has a lot of responsibility. It's not just about saying "Do this, do that," and develop education; it is also about social, political, economic development and we have to come together for this kind of planning as well. Thank you.

MELİH BARUT: Professor Nacos, I see that you would like to add some new comments.

BRIGITTE L. NACOS: Nothing would change. You could pump anything, you can do a lot of education. Boko Haram is against education by itself. They are kidnaping people from schools so that they cannot learn, particularly the girls. So, I do not think any development would help that. What is true is that if you have development, distribution of resources then maybe in the future people will not be recorded. But a lot of people are just with ISIS, and they are being forced into it, they are not running happily into their arms. Unfortunately, I believe that you have to win the fight against terrorist organization by talking the language they would understand. Education, and fair distribution of the resources would surely work thereafter.

MELİH BARUT: As for the last comment from your side. Professor Karlığa, please go ahead.

BEKİR KARLIĞA: Yes, I am of course taking into consideration what you say, I understand. But as educators, I believe that we have to communicate to these people as well. We have to reach out to them as well to be able to consider them as humans. I understand what you say and yes, their extremism has some reason for them and I still think we can reach out to them through some sort of educational activities and we would be able to somehow relieve that environment.

MELİH BARUT: Thank you very much for the comments. All right, before I close this panel discussion, actually this beautiful conversation, I would like to thank everyone who made this effort happen both from Cultural Diplomacy Academy of Yunus Emre Institute and Global Public Diplomacy Network as well. Also many special thanks goes to the presidency and representatives of Global Public Diplomacy Network members, candidate countries, observers, and to the distinguished guests, I mean to you, the audience.

I would also like to thank everyone who participated in this process both in the back and front stage. So, I don't want to count the names because we are so many. Especially, I would like to thank for the diligent efforts that

Yunus Emre Institute personal executed lately. Thank you very much. And finally, I would like to thank to Professor Nacos, she is my academic mother and mentor actually, Professor Karlığa and my dear friend Ambassador Luis Palma. So, from here I have a small advice to Ambassador Palma. He is very tired, he came all the way from Chile to Turkey for this special event after 18 hours of flight and in the meantime his luggage was lost during transfers, too. My advice to him: Please, next time fly with Turkish Airlines. Thank you very much for being with us.

We will be looking forward to meeting with you in the next Yunus Emre Institute Cultural Diplomacy Academy and Global Public Diplomacy Network conference.

www.ingramcontent.com/pod-product-compliance
Lightning Source LLC
Chambersburg PA
CBHW040828300326
41914CB00059B/1261